TENDER REASONS

POEMS

Joseph Jeremy

REGENT PRESS
Berkeley, California

Copyright © 2014 by Joseph Jeremy

[paperback]
ISBN 13: 978-1-58790-257-4
ISBN 10: 1-58790-257-5
Library of Congress Catalog Number: 2013954299

PHOTO: James Garrahan *artist/photographer*

Manufactured in the U.S.A.

REGENT PRESS
Berkeley, California
www.regentpress.net

Yellow roses, Spanish guitars, nights full of rain,
summer clouds-these are some of the characters in
this book. The sea, certain woman who haunt, make quick
appearances in between the rain. If these letters and poems
don't break down and cry, it is not their fault maybe they
        should.
It's just that if you've ever visited wonder, the night, stars,
moonlight, like moonlight was the treasure.

Contents

I

Song	2
London	3
San Anselmo	4
Paradise	5

II

Back When	8
So Soft	11
I Wake Up	12
I Owe You An Apology	14
The Carpet, The Overstuffed Chairs	16
(For M)	17
V	18
VI	20
The Grand Condradiction	21
A Man Sits	22

III

Time	24
From a Notebook	27
Guardian	28
Sausalito Breakdown	29
VII	30

IV

The Garden	32
Her Eyes	34
Meditation	36
The Reign	37
Wondering	39

INVISIBLE	41
WHAT WERE THE CLOUDS LIKE?	42
LUNA	45
A PALE BLUE TOWEL	46

V

ANNO DOMINI	48
WE ARE MEANT TO FIND	50
ON STOPPING TO STUDY AN OAK	51
ROOT	52
LOST IN YOUR HAIR	53
FROM A NOTEBOOK	54
TIME	55
ANOTHER LIFE	57

VI

THAT GIRL	60
THE PROFUSION OF NATURE	61
LIBERER	62
BOOKS	63
BLUE JAY	64
TAO	65
TO BE ANONYMOUS	66
NOVEMBER	67
FLIGHT	69
CARMEL	70

VII

HOMAGE	72
LEGENDS	73
THE REPORT	74
COURTING THE MUSE	75
A PERFECT DAY, GIVEN THE SEA	76
SPRING	77

SHE LEANED OVER	78
JEAN	80
THERE'S NO THERE THRERE	82
LIZARD	84
NOVEL	85
FEBRUARY	87
THE 7TH MUSE	88
THE DAY	91
BLUE CORDUROYS	92
THE MOON	94

VIII

A FOGGY DAY	96
ROSSELL	97
LOVE	98
DANCING	99
CONFESSION	100
IT WASN'T SO MUCH DANCING FOR HOURS	101
WITH OR WITHOUT	102
THE SEA	103
JULY	104

I

Song

The hum of bicycles going by,
thongs on pavement,
sound of a blue dress
subtle and difficult to hear.

Lunch, the destination
on a terrace overlooking boats
standing in line for sandwiches
her hair just washed.

A sparrow
briefly on a branch,
beyond that hundreds of white masts,
the sea not asking for attention
except to reflect, dazzling
just past her shoulder
suggesting what the afternoon might do.

What possibility
in a cluster of clouds
as if time had lost track of us,
as if the wind, these leaves
could be written down, each movement,
each flutter of tablecloth.

I recognize this wind,
why it picks an afternoon
like this.
So just a light breeze
to be cupped in the hand
and saved.

London

Still searching early on a Sunday
walking through Kensington Gardens
alongside the fountains, the flowers,
the gentle goddess that surely hides there
leaning over the railings-a thousand white English daisies.
Details of the old London moon, broken,
floating through the purple sky.
An open window, churches, medieval faces,
no sign of the goddess. Was she hiding
in the stain glass window?
Was she in the archways?
Thinking real written history would be the history
of gentleness, kisses, perfumes, quick embraces,
glances, closed doors, instead of battles and executions.
What is interesting is not who destroyed
who (which we have in great detail), but who
loved who. There should be great shrines
made to people who loved.

"We don't go to the tea shops" she said
"You must put on your own kettle."
She was England with her blue eyes
leaning near a door originating in the Fifteenth century.
Five hundred years of sun, rain, wind…aware
of that walking through the small villages, lingering
outside the old forgotten estates. Padding the huge walls,
sitting in the cafes, with the open windows
admiring some green carnations, two green carnations
to be exact and a dark haired English waitress bending
slightly towards us like the old trees across the way,
the graves with no one thinking of hiding them
just there under the trees, framing them with your eyes,
like painters painting them, slowly, gently, the English graves.

San Anselmo

It's very much like being there when you're in love:
The candles, the silence after she says something.
To have her under the stars means the muses
are almost too kind. To have this brown haired nymph
next to you at midnight in a strange town
watching a classic early John Wayne film you've both
seen before, and there were sliced peaches
and coffee earlier and the different angles of sitting and
lying in front of a television set knowing the risks, the last
saga, portrait, details of a painting (When you do enter, again,
the museum studying the old paints, the canvases,
  the other summers.)
When bravery and foolishness become each other or
  when the risk
is necessary, when you have to live knowing the dangers.
  Knowing
that kissing her under the stars, holding her in the backyard
under the trees with no moon is incredibly dangerous
but you have been blind along time now. You know blindness.
It is one of the trails.

Paradise

A place in the imagination though
echoing from the everyday, it nevertheless
reigns supreme.

A personal place
it can be shared.

A living room used as a library,
big cushioned couches,
a fireplace roaring behind its metal screen.

A few moments,
a few minutes,
a few hours, days, weeks, years
spent loving.

A few moments
spent loving.
That's all.

II

Back When

I

Back when
you spent
great amounts

of time
teaching the moth
about the flame,

that life
was not a race,
that time

would have
ideas
of her own

know
the real fields
you would be tilling

when
there was no time
nothing

to mark you
distinctions
made out of thin air,

the highest rank
found
in the most obscure

places
like the nests
of birds
or the path
of the smallest
field mouse

following
in the furrows
of a plow.

II

Weeks
staring out
small windows

singing
to the sparrows,
the eucalyptus,

old deteriorated barns
just past
the willow trees,

wind
whipping the fence posts,
the force

that allowed you
to keep on
paying

tributes
to the abandoned
flowers.

That there
are too few
singers,
too few
delicious moments
of happiness

that should be
shouted
from the rooftops.

So Soft

Spring cottages, tall weeds,
flowers climbing over windows,
places only a few would have dared…
Red wing blackbirds
low over the fields
singing in their metallic voices
as if they knew the blossoms,
the wind through tall grass,
symphony conductors,
wings smoothing over the afternoon,
the wind
full of legends,
full of those who lived before,
who knew how to kneel.

I Wake Up

I wake up in my own bed
in the middle of the night
having lived here thirteen years
and I still don't know where I am.
I'm not sure many of us know where we are
or how we got there.
Whitman said: the only thing that matters
the great souls.

It does not have to be said anymore, it's true.
The only thing that matters: the great moments,
the rare narrow pathway to someone else.
Night is almost here.
I look out: small white farm houses
even rows of apple trees, gray horizon,
Time has just continued through the Nineteenth,
the Twentieth century like a painting, a Van Gogh.
As for the struggle. The incredible unspeakable struggle.
There is nothing but silence.
The conspiracy is so well in tact,
so masterly put together hardly any ones aware.
The moment has been stolen. Taken away
and what's put in its place is some vague glamorized future,
some vague guilt of not quite being right, you see, there
can only be a few great positions (This is what has been so
        perfectly taught),
which keeps everyone trying and hoping mortgaging their
        lives till
all you can see is this kind of disappointment, this kind of
        broken dream
when the pathetic part is its not even their dream

that's broken, its someone elses something they were
>	handed.

It's embarrassing to say but you are already there.
Now, here, in just that light, in this chair, wearing these
>	clothes.
It's not going to be next week or next year or after this or
>	that
or when thats finally paid for
or when you fimilly make this or that decision
or whatever the inspired contingencies…

I Owe You An Apology

The only thing, I suppose, that I didn't emphasize
was that you would have to pay some kind of price
for being a writer, for studying poetry, for hanging out
in cafes and reading French existentialists, for the apprenticeship.
I couldn't have known what the prices would be, but
in a materialistic society they run high.
Poets are not looked on kindly by those
who spend years in the banks, advancing their careers,
probably because a serious poet has is own world
and his accounts cannot be measured in the usual way
and also because expression is not a value (except for the very
    few).
You find out that the world doesn't have the patience
for a poet to develop himself. Good poets develop over time
and since there just isn't time, there isn't a number of years
set aside for one to experience and learn language,
learn how to express oneself, there aren't going to be many poets.
They would have to be on the endangered species list.
Post Modernism: even if you establish your identity (which is
    no small feat)
your audience is going to be small, almost microscopic.
You may have known all this. Maybe after you discovered how
incredibly lonely it was out in the world, after you saw the
    other arena.
The endless buildings and disappointments, you wondered why
you haddn't been building your empire, why it was just sand
    and dust
around you. The owners own the world. Now if you buy into
    that,
if you evaluate life on that scale, you better be an owner.
        Otherwise

by definition you end up like our mutual friend
convinced that he doesn't belong, convinced
he's no good. And by their standards his interpretation is correct.
Don't tell anybody what I'm about to say but the owners don't
    own anything.
What they own are masks. Well built, even artistic, maybe
    even dazzling
but just masks, assertions, barricades…It's a grand illusion,
    the conspiracy is intact.
There is just a few of us who have caught on. Who do not
    want to trade.
Give me a cold gray afternoon in March with hundreds of
    apple trees.
Let me talk with them. Let them whisper about the petals,
how much the angle of a branch might be worth, what the
    color of the sky
and the yellow mustard…

The Carpets, The Overstuffed Chairs

The carpets, the overstuffed chairs, the stars,
the chance to find something beautiful.
If all you will be left with is "the beautiful moments,"
the final parting when you look over your life
and ask how much graciousness was in it. How many times
you loved it just because it was a scene.

Sitting in a favorite haunt of mine
just west of the university,
(One of my mythologies is being
an assoicate professor in Ancient Roman history
living in a small apartment secretly convinced
it's still Rome twenty three hundred years ago.)
I found a table in the sunlight...
Dark green corduroys, blue Roos Atkins shirt,
penny loafers, gray socks,

a copy of the German philosopher Martin Heidegger's
book (Dedicated in friendship and admiration
to Edmund Husserl, April, nineteen twenty-six.)
Italian english speaking students all around me
carrying notebooks, empty white chair on my right:
yours ghost sitting there browsing through an
      F. Scott Fitzgerald story
I found a table in the sunlight,
in the French sunlight, the Belgian sunlight (This refers
to a complicated European theory I wont go into here.)
Another leaf drops off from a tree, shadows of remaining
leafs dance across the table. It is almost winter.

(for M.)

Various notes from the birds
since there is still the sun.
As if each of them were grateful,
almost joyous.

It all fits so well:
trees, grass, the ivy growing.
Are you there too conducting the warm afternoon?
Your presence in the very clouds?

What luck to still live in the palace
knowing the storeroom only too well.
Days of grace
when the blinds part just enough

And one can see beyond the treetops,
knows the provisions, the outlines of infinity.
You are the dream
while the dream lasts.

V

Lying in the sand kissing,
the next morning
he moved in.
Sleeping bags
covered in fog,
three pancakes by a window,
a sleepy waitress
who hadn't woken up yet.

The field
mostly rabbits
that winter, tufts of weed.
They could see it
from their bedroom window
full of mud, innocence,
that indifference
a landscape has.

The cemetery
so close it became
part of their walk.
Rain, fog,
windy nights,
uneven tombstones
ragged and quiet
stars on a clear night.

Free
in a world of slaves
or that's how
he pictured them.

Actually they too
were slaves to the moon,
late nights
out across the field,

to other less obvious things.
Slaves
in their twenties,
what was it for
but to love someone
there
after midnight
like some grand obsession.

VI

She on the quiet side
kept to herself
muttering incantations
to the winter rain.

He obsessed with the dead,
the tiny cemetery
he would take her in for walks late at night,
sit on the old tombstones and wonder:

"Jane Oliver, 1870-1942,"
a whole life in two lines.
A crescent moon
shining down from the heavens...

They knew enough to savor the treasure,
linger over it
as if it were a dare
as he noticed a few strands of hair

out of place over the ears,
over a conversation
about doing exactly what you want,
live it like this is it.

Not tomorrow
or in some vague future
plan but here in front of your eyes
without a crown.

The Grand Contradiction

The grand contradiction
Handed from generation
to generation:
one can live in the world
incredibly happy
if one ignores "the rules."

Ghosts,
windy afternoons,
Russian novels,
Anna Karenina walking along the path
to the bookstore,
French philosophers,

does it have to have a beginning,
a middle and an end?
Couldn't there
just be these characters
turning aside, blinking,
full of wonder.

The end of summer.
Are there still those
who count their lives by summers?

A Man Sits

A man sits at a table facing a bare wall.
There is a calender.
The table he sits at does not move, the wall,
the man himself does not move but somehow
there are vast cities in his imagination, theaters,
revolutions, characters he has given
the finest awards to (Pulitzer prize winning eyes).

Candlelight by the sea, quarter moon
Conversations that were not particularly notable
In what was said but in the breathing, in the silence
between the spoken words, the light from the candles.
It was all contained in the dreams they had: faded pastels,
silk scarfs, orchestrations of a long blue dress,
a Roman muse he had re-named in a long dress
on the steps of the temple.

Isn't it possible we forgot (This idea haunts him).
That we were allowed in so often, on so many occasions
that we came to expect it with the same frequency
and therein lies our malaise.
It is only appreciation we have to study.

III

Time

I
The sets
endless as the days,
the clouds say in Italy or Spain.
Coffee, yellow roses on a table,
candlelight, the glance
before dessert when she laughed
(Had she laughed
when you'd mentioned the fight
with the windmills?)

Her appearance on the page there
among the white parchment
and what meaning would it have?
The wind would rise higher
and faster along the sea wall
and you would go with it
knowing desire,
how longing can be like the beginning
of winter.

II
What will you find
driving through the night?
Enough patience
to look at the stars
or the discovery
that the road is endless,
that you know nothing
driving down this road
the great night affirming this.

You will learn again
to love,
remember the silence
eyes looking at you
so delicate
and you will continue on
through the night, the night
who is a better note taker
than you.

III
Feeling
there isn't much time
when there is,
a glance outside
every tree, field,
shows how stationary,
how endlessly stationary
but there is a different rhythm
in the human heart.

We may not
be able to comprehend
a row of apple trees
a few scattered apples.
How to understand
something
that doesn't move,
just endlessly available
to the seasons.

IV
To wander at night,
wonder what the stars are doing,
what process hides so well behind the light.
Yesterday in the cafe realizing the less mystery
we allow the older we become.
Even the most hardened
among us looks out occasionally
questioning where or why or just what
got him down the road this far.

V
Two by fours,
planks of pine,
sanding, re-finishing small windows
secret doors that lead to rooms
so you could remember
the smell of her,
the way to hold her
when she moved in the night.

VI
A particular fence post.
A past that will not
call you back
unless you want to go
unless you never left.

From A Notebook

All day in the cafe
lost in a kind of timelessness
as if it were the Fifties again
or the Sixties instead of 05 in the century
2000.
…
Eating carrots, sipping green tea,
Looking out at the terrace, the blue sky,
the trees. "Make it new" Pound said
as if it wasn't already.
…
A poem by Kenneth Rexroth (1952):
                           We believed we
Would see with our own eyes the new
World where man was no longer
Wolf to man, but men and women
Were all brothers and lovers
Together. We will not see it.
We will not see it, none of us.
It is farther off than we thought
… It does not matter.
We were comrades together.
Life was good for us. It is
Good to be brave — nothing is
Better. Food tastes better. Wine
Is more brilliant. Girls are more
Beautiful. The sky is bluer…
If the good days never come,
We will not know. We will not care.
Our lives were the best. We were the
Happiest men alive in our day.

Guardian

Living on
in various cars,
rooms,
through how many winters?

(And he saying it hadn't worked.)

Did he mean
when the sheets
were pulled down,
the pillows put in place?

The kisses,
late night conversations?
Did he mean
all the laughter hadn't worked?

Rooms we sat in
hundreds of times
staring at each other?
Did he mean each time we made love?

SAUSALITO BREAKDOWN

They talk of the beginning
They talk of the end,
but I talk of now

The view of the leather jacket
the smell of it.
As I sit at my desk. Women
& gold spun out of nothing.
One women in particular,
two hundred and eighty-five…
gold pieces…

I talk of the sea, the forest.

VII

Her presence had a way of lingering
like the wild flowers
outside my door
until she arrived
until
again…

"What if
it's only a dream,"
we would say
walking up
the paths
of the moon.

All night in the cafe,
writing long letters
not knowing how others love,
I had only my instincts,
only the song
of her knock on the door.

Long hair,
turned up nose,
conversations (What was they to say?),
preparing dinner,
lighting the fire, anonymous
as any small cottage in August.

O Maggie,
whisper to me
of the legends
only a few got to live.
Tell me again of the flowers
that grow wild under the moon.

IV

The Garden

A blonde and brunette laughing
sitting next to one another.
You can't remember what about,
only that they were laughing
as if laughter itself was an old Roman song
carried down through the ages.

The blonde was older,
from a whole different part of the country
but never mind.
They were sisters. Both in love with you.
You weren't sure what love was
but had signed the contract
and paid the taxes and other costs
necessary and the blonde had agreed.
It wasn't a huge sum
but in those days
even small amounts were precious.

You had offered to pay for the brunette too
but only casually in conversation
with your eyes and she had accepted
(with her eyes),
but when it was put to you bluntly
that you take her upstairs
and live with her,
make that small bed, the little view
of the stars and the moon… You realized
the cost of the trade. Her long hair,
quick laughter, her nineteen year old smirk
would take too much financing.

Long afterwards you would wonder
if you made the right decision,
if you shouldn't have signed.
That afternoon in the garden
amongst all the laughter when you bent down
and carried the blonde up the stairs
so gently, so impossible she was
insisting on full examinations, handling
every part like it was crystal, like
it had been handed down from mother to daughter:
it was a matter of care, finally,
you had been knighted.

Her Eyes

Her eyes,
what moments to be classified in the encyclopedia
under music
on the linoleum in the afternoon in the kitchen or just
        driving out to the sea
as if her hair was the reason, as if to study the light,
on the dashboard, the turns in the road,
the simple fact you are still alive,
that you and this drive and this woman
are all perfectly obscure, perfectly camouflaged,
who would want to know that you kissed?
That the light made a perfect triangle
On the dashboard, that you are not living
In the real world measuring your life
in afternoons, lipstick.
Together on the bed talking,
knowing you could spend the whole afternoon
watching the blue curtains,
listening to the silence, the movement of the dust.
Islands . . . .*It is almost the end of July. The workforce
is through with their coffee break.*
There are only a few of us quietly doing paperwork.
Much like work at an embassy on a Wednesday
only the work refers to legends, nights of Bach,
nights full of rain, long dissertations
tracing the path of an elbow, eyelashes,
a pair of sandals.
There are more of us that are recorded, secret codes
still abound, a glance in this direction
from a pair of eyes — could this be a part of it?
It is a hipness that would not have a word today.

It is better we don't have names for it. Unspeakable
conversations now, here where you are unmentioned
except in the way she walks down the hall. The rareness
of a creature who believes she has already arrived —
Not later or afterwards or when but here already
in this chair drinking a cappuccino.
It is more often to be found in women, this gentleness,
this direct caring about the world.
The Spanish guitar on a night when it would not stop
      raining,
when plans to share a kitchen together was possible,
A conversation about "idenity," "titles" people carry
that do not make them happy, that make it possible for
      them to hide,
to not be obvious. For finally, the obviousness of a life can get
to be too much. That you exist
can push in on you with much pressure and
there is a great relief inside a word surrounded with
tradition and institutions though it does not bring happiness.
The structures that provide this relief are just outlines,
      forms,
mere echoes of what you thought might protect you..
Nothing will protect you. The necessity in
      understanding this,
the negotiations
that occur in the midnight hour or perhaps alone
in the morning, a great tenderness.
So, you speak while sitting in front of the fire.
You speak about understanding from a different level.
There is a great longing to identify the distinct
countries in those eyes-errings flashing in the firelight —
The apprenticeship has begun.

Meditation

In front of a mirror,
an aging character actor

no reason to hope
to be taken seriously
now.

There is a smuggler loose,
perhaps in the night,
perhaps only in dreams
but he or she is
loose.

Why aren't there
more celebrations,
More dancing in the streets?

That the curtains
are being tugged at
even as we speak.

The Reign

You wanted to memorize,
weave like some mad weaver
all the ecstasies
like the moon reflected
in the small mirror last night.
That afternoon near an old barn
thinking the entire afternoon could be
devoted to this modest position:

sunlight, in the dust by the little bridge
a few feet from the road.
A road Romans might have walked down.
You closed your eyes and you were anywhere,
then focused on the barn.
Nine hundred years had passed.
What complications could arise from this simplicity:
walls, rivers, bridges that looked so much

like the holy wars and the eleventh century,
you could see the crosses, the black and white helmets.
Pages and pages of notes
to compose a score,
choreograph the moonlight,
those of us who still frequent the cafes
and study the blue charts.
Rest on old broken walls, feel the sea,

time,
not much changed since the Greeks.
Thirty mile an hour winds all night listening
to the metal shutters clashing.

Black hooded sweatshirts
against the wind,
steep mountain roads, dazzling blue designs
between the sails.

Approaching mid-night, mid-life:
are the dreams
in your twenties and thirties
different from the ones in your
forties and fifties?
By a roaring fire.
The fog having come in again.
You dream the same dreams.

The wind these past afternoons
illustrating time, moving everything
that has happened and everything that will
into trees swaying.
You take a dark night, a wind and then the sea,
a life that has been many love affairs,
a wind that lives them over and over
as if there were only broken walls dividing them,

the sea crashing.
Dawn, dangerous and cold
but perfect
from the front seat of a car,
perfect
with Bach on the radio,
fragile
and perfect.

Wondering

Devoting ones's self to the morning light,
to capture what it means to grow old,
wear wool sweaters…
Wasn't it just as it should have been?
Moments you held her
neither of you free from old ghosts,
still chained to the outlines of people
you had made into legends.

Winter light by a window
just the sounds the trees
seem to be making
in the rain,
just the slope of the hill
and how would one be able to sit and dream
of these things,
what ancient privileges.

Each of us his own historian
making his own notes
(However brief),
arranging the photographs of the battle.
Each could tell the exact
formation of the clouds
that afternoon,
the direction of the wind.

(If they have stopped remembering,
if they stop bringing out
the old notebooks,
if an early death…)

Is it possible to still be in love,
lie out under the stars
and compose mad songs,
etch the people you will always love
(quietly leaves gather in the wind,
each leaf appointed to rest there
in just that way… a winter royalty.)

Invisible

Some of the characters
have changed in your play,
some will always be
just off the wings
knowing their time, but then,
we might have to forget
all about time.

The past is here now.
its invisibility is our blindness.
A first kiss
a first flight of delight, laughter,
a process whereby we started
no bigger than a thumbnail
and will end up lowered down
slowly into a grave
to be carried about the heavens.
...
Somewhere between Tarifa and Algeciras now
spending the afternoon
on a Spanish beach:
sand, wind, certain seabirds.
There is only this growing feeling of luck.
Able to lie here and dream,
imagine centuries of seabirds
that must have traveled
up and down this coast,
who knew nothing of the words "the Alboran Sea"
they had just crossed from Africa,
who knew no words,
just wings and wind,
gray and white feathers.

What Were the Clouds Like?

Huge land masses circulating,
the smallest blue sky
between swirls, the wind visible,,,

Was she there?
Yes. Quiet, scared.

And?
No more, just the sound of the tires
on the road,
the engine.

There were kisses?
I suppose.

You were in love.
Yes.

Even though?
Despite the fact that she wouldn't
answer most of the questions.

You were cross-examing her?
I wanted to find out
what myths she's been living.

And she wouldn't tell you?
She couldn't.
Most of the time she would look down
at the floor or rest her head on an elbow…

This woman who had no idea what she wanted,
where she was going
meant everything to you?
Yes.

You lived in three rooms?
Yes.

She was writing a book on middle english?

Chaucer. She didn't know why.
Her mother had sent her to the country.
We burned all her Chaucer books.

You made her destroy her work?
She didn't care.
You have to understand. There was no time.
She thought there was.

You mean future?
Yes. I taught her there wasn't going
to be a future. She couldn't count on it.
As long as something else could happen later,
she could live with Chaucer, sleep with Chaucer,
make endless notes on what he might have meant,
weave it all into an endless speculation
on the dark ages, step out of her life
and into another with a man who'd been dead
for almost eight hundred years.

She understood all this?
There were other things.

She would make hot apple pies
in the middle of the night.
There was something in her eyes, something
that said she didn't know but wanted to.
It's not easy to describe. She'd never known anyone
with a myth before.

A myth?
A series of sacred things he believed in,
a mythology actually lived: heroes, legends.
She had only known your average myth-less
knight who wanted to carry her off
to a loft somewhere, pound on his breastplate,
lost in a world that had already been explained
and fully mapped. A world with a king. She'd never
known anyone who had created his own king.

Luna

What could you tell someone
who wasn't there?
That the moon was full and you
were on your knees in that field?
Do you say she was a simple peasant,
that she was shy and there are few records.
Can you explain fragileness,
when you could not speak,
afraid of breaking the spell.
Ancient caves in the barest of light
far from the battles.
Conducting secret orchestras,
unheard of music.

A Pale Blue Towel

A pale blue towel
hangs
on the bed post.
Sometimes
aroumd her,
sometimes falling
to the floor,
at the foot of the bed,
on a chair.

It is Saturday
but only the newspapers
and calanders
will support this conspiracy.
And the pale blue towel?
Does it speak?
Will it tell where it's been
in its cotton world?
What histories of arms and legs,
unspeakable nights
that must be sung,
lie folded and quiet
like nothing ever happened.

V

Anno Domini

Writing this while driving forty miles
an hour crossing a long span bridge…
should take me into Marin.
My green toothbrush presently stationed
in silver cup on shelf in her bathroom.
The cup was her christening cup "June 19,
1958," etched in black.

Yesterday at breakfast:
"How does it feel to be on top of my list"?
The French congress had just sent
a messenger to inform Napoleon
he'd been appointed emperor of France.
My new sweater folded neatly in her closet.
My black fur hat
just covering her economics book.

I've stopped the truck.
In cafe now just long enough to sit,
imagine how Monet might have painted her
sleeping between the pillows,
how he would have outlined her hair,
the long Sunday afternoons, her nipples
in the Hiltons' coffee shop, the fountain.
It's all happened so fast. My desk
moved in alongside hers, clothes hanging
in between her clothes, our books scattered
in piles. She told me Chopin's music has been
in the background since we met.

Another long Sunday afternoon and she's right,
Chopin has been accompanying us. A windshield
covered in rain, yesterday the sea, watching
from a table overlooking a small harbor,
a thousand white masts, time running as if
it had nothing to do with us, the sound of cars
in the street, older ladies nearby in white hair
whispering words like "reminisce."

We walk across the square
still half asleep, still half back in our room,
the Peruvian lilies bending towards the window,
Chopin's ballad number four played so often
it hangs from the ceiling, our clothes
folded neatly as if it wasn't us living there,
not our fingerprints on the windows, not
our faces reflcected in the mirrors
but some ancient couple living
on the outskirts of Rome.

We Are Meant to Find

We are meant to Find
It's a long apprenticeship and often without a guide
But these stars, this black night
what is it but some exquisite dance,
some play of the wind that refuses to unmask herself,
that weaves much more masterfully
than our own imaginations.
Who could invent the moon?

On Stopping To Study An Oak

Staring up at the top
of the tree, leaves pointing
at various angles
(I almost said angels).

Wondering how it was here
all night with the moon
and then the dawn
branches pointing

towards heaven, outstretched arms,
castle for squirrels,
place for almost anything
to live, rest, and then

thousands of them lining
the hillsides and the mountains
like sentries
guarding the night.

Root

The root
of our suffering
is that we are slaves…

How successful the masters
to keep you
from knowing…
Of course, because we'd leave,
how could we keep on
working with figures that mean nothing,
how could we keep on buying.

"You're going to carry that weight
along time."
They write songs about it.
Guarded so perfectly
(like any
great thing).

We have been taught (0 citizens).
We believe…
and who is this for,
finally.

(They have stolen the moment.)

LOST IN YOUR HAIR

Lost in your hair I was never lost
enough to lose my direction.

Lost in your hair I was never lost
except in the sense of being far off
like being on this island
southern breezes, full sun,

no more than building a monument,
a statue…

From a Notebook

In the wind, the voices…
…
And so for one who is a master
at pleasure, the little things
are likewise ritualized (worshiped).
…
The wheel — how does one get off?
By realizing
any point on the wheel is there.
…
An upstairs apartment,
midnight wearing her usual black stockings
some ancient myth
like Troy had just fallen.
Were you Agamemnon? Hector?
She had tacked a poem of yours

just above her pillow
or was it you she had tacked up:
a bit of feathers from your helmet,
a bronze medallion from a sandal,
notes from a song you had played
on the lyre.

Her mouth tight like Helen's mouth,
a Greek mouth
in the desperate kingdom of love.

Time

"My sky blue trades"
                — Dylan Thomas

Choosing to be free,
to be alone,
and then if he worships…

How can this be explained:
the afternoon, the sky,
wandering through clouds,

long hours studying
"The great gifts
are not got by analysis,"

or "Absolute abandonment."
He's running his own revolution
yet no one has to know.

All quietly taking place
inside a man's mind.
Lives his little time,

basks in what he alone
is fortunate enough to find
chanting "Blessed be nothing,"

we are all in chains
he repeats to himself,
do not kid yourself

but there are different brands
made of different material.
Some

are just tied up with rope.
Some
have made their own.

Another Life

Flowers
Along an embankment,
a lake
somewhere in the mountains

(Should I have mentioned these?) .
The train
I forgot to get on,
Where it went

Whether I could have conversations
Over coffee and scones
Looking into your eyes
And dreaming

Not of another life
But how original this one,
Each frame,
Each compartment,

Nights sleeping next to you
The wind roaming
around
Like it wanted in

Like it had something
To do with the train
Why there was no stopping,
I still see

The color
of the pillowcases
Reflected in the train's
windows.

I should
Have mentioned the night,
That we came from it
That we're headed back

Telling you with my eyes
As I leaned out the window
of another
train.

You couldn't possibly
have known
or guessed
my accommodations

Now
as if the long night
had us both…
Lights

reflected
for a moment
in your eyes.

VI

THAT GIRL

To wait so long for that blonde to appear in your life.

At twenty-nine she arrived. (And stayed until I was almost thirty.)

What more can one desire? Nine, ten months seems like nineteen,

Twenty years. If time can be repressed, seconds made more intense,

Hours vanishing like days, weeks. It was all so fast but lasted so long.

I can still smell her…the back of her neck, her breasts. It was being

So familiar with anothers body it never left. These twenty years

emblazoned … It is only gratitude we have to learn…

The Profusion of Nature

The trees are everywhere, leaves
blowing in the wind, growth.

The borders are constantly being crossed.
The appealing fact of it…like you're almost

being embraced, caressed in the afternoon
by the trees.

Liberer

Traveling
from sunset to sunset,
particles
of Roman dust
in a suitcase,
a few daisies,
irretrievably lost
a concept Lawrence
worked on for years,
Flaubert.

There are the strong
and the weak.
The weak
put the cross down gently,
Let it rest there.
No one will bother it.
Life can be
so complicated
on so many levels
yet so simple.

A Roman woman
wearing white
throwing her arms up
illustrating
that not much
has changed
since Roman times,
still woman in doorways
comers to sit
and compose songs.

Books

Books and books of thought, emotion, opinion,
the lost and the found. All piled up on my shelves.
Forgotten lines, remembered ones, so many, so few.
Borges, Rexroth, Neruda, Brodsky, Stevens, Padilla,
Pound, Rilke, Creeley. Like the sand on a beach.

Blue Jay

High in the trees
black rivet eyes
flash in the sunlight,
slash of silver penciled in
where an eyebrow
could have been.

Last of it
in the upper branches
as if devoted,
as if it owed something
to this light,
this last bit of heat.

Proud in her world
as she moves her head,
flutters her wings.
Last of the sun worshipers
appearing at the dutiful hour
knowing what is expected

which twig to rest on.
O little one, do I sense
a whisper of immortality?
Something beautiful
and completely impossible.
The dust on your wings from the leaves.

Tao

Sitting all day
In the cafe
reading Watts *The Watercourse Way*
Eating lemon cake,

drinking coffee,
lost in the definition of the Tao.
Looking out over the sea now
from my desk.

Wondering, the sea doesn't distinguish
itself as "'Tuesday's sea,"
does it?
It's just the wild sea, any day.

An in-board ship goes by
raising waves.
It's a great backdrop the sea,
the broad empty sea.

To Be Anonymous

"Famous among the barns"
                    — Dylan Thomas

To be anonymous.
The greatness in obscurity.
Late afternoon in the study
tree shapes, a hill down to some water,
fading sunlight, fame hidden
in the most remote comers,
in the most average of circumstances.
Gradually darkness descends.

November

A manuscript
thrown
In the back of a plane,

New York in the dead of winter.
Almost Thanksgiving
snow falling,

a cold office
the academy rented
for the aging prize-winning

New York judge poet.
The work will stand
or fall by itself,

perhaps it should be standing
or falling in the Greek islands
or in southern France

(which you were fortunate
enough to do a walking tour
in some years ago)

or possibly even a desert,
a small manuscript left alone
out in the middle of the Sahara....

But why not
an aging snow covered judge
who may understand

those who want to sing.
It is a wonder
but there's plenty of wonder,

whole palaces of it as Emerson said:
and thou shalt possess that wherin others
are only tenants and boarders.

Flight

Bright stems of yellow (Van Gogh) mustard
in a clump alongside the road.
Coastal breeze,
reading signs of an osprey's flight,
eating fresh shrimp,
talking of inland life
how a rose (pink)
might be written in
as the central part of the script,
a cottage
also still standing
ivy, trees, shrubs,
an entire orchard still left in the mind
like that osprey gliding
just above water,
like memory.

Carmel (Dec. 5, 2006)

On the beach.

The sound of the sea from the room.
Stretched out on the bed listening.
Lost in it: receding, crashing, crashing, receding.
Distant but somehow close by. The mystery
of the sea.

Put on my black loafers, out for the sunset.

My obsessions are waning:
automobiles, cigarettes, clothes…

A drive down highway one to Big Sir
under the dazzling sun.

VII

Homage

Sunset clings to the hills, abandoning the terrace
but the coffee has gone cold, or is finished, a gnat hums.
Her light wool sweater makes Serena look grander than ever.
Her starched cotton blouse is buttoned up to her neck.
Samantha nodding from the comer as she reads
from a yellow paperback.

Our four rooms remain silent in response to the willows.
Venus sparkles in a violet sky masquerading as herself
for the millionth time. The puppy chews on a sock.
As the rooms darken there are notes
still hidden under a magazine.
The statues will remain long after

the two woman are gone, crumbling but still leaving their shapes.
"Who's cooking dinner?" Serena will say knowing anyway.
Afterwards, "Ole blue eyes" sings songs
all our mothers would remember.
Outside it will start to rain but barely. ~
The frogs in the garden singing their notes.

What will become of me, Serena wonders watching the shade
from the lamp.
What will the night make of me, she thinks
as the willows sway with the wind
and the new rain.

The puppy nestling closer to the heater.
The night so eternal in its tuxedo,
so deep as Samantha reaches for an edge of the blanket
and Serena stares up at the ceiling unable to sleep,
while the notes are still under the magazine
writing themselves.

Legends

Long afternoons
of nothing more ambitious
than the sky, a few clouds,
the form of a hill, the sound
down among the cliffs, a world
of utter sky blue simplicity.
I haven't lost the sense of that dream.
It can be moved about and carried
even in the most complicated
of situations.

There was a point, and not just in love,
but in the everyday sense, when there
were beautiful legendary evenings,
when the sea was laughing,
when the idea of myth was enough of an explanation,
when money by itself was an accomplishment
(even small amounts). The elaborate facade
was not so much things, as made up of the imagination.
The enemy was more of a sense of something
 than anything bothered to be defined.

It has been a matter of finding the sun
at dawn, to locate it by itself as important
and then collect these "dawns" along with
sunsets, Gaugain prints, flowers alongside
the road, myths that required great strength
to even attempt. The essential thing is to know
that you may not arrive, even though you have
trained youself to see. So, one must be content
In wanting to collect the colors of the dawn in his notebook,
in just the wanting.

The Report

The trees surround me.
There is a half moon tonight.
The moon is like an accompaniment,
It follows where ever you go.
I'll call this the Sausalito moon
as it stares back from the west window.
The moon which has been looked at
by so many
it is a lover.

Courting The Muse (for E.D.)

He enters his study,
the tiled floor hardly notices,
the blinds, the lamp,
the small turkish carpet…

Two cats sleep side by side nearby
dreaming of nothing in particular.
They too are vaguely aware
of his existence.

The books stand quietly on their shelves,
the rattan chair in the far corner
still carries creases
of when he visited.

She is there but requires
a certain kind of attention,
as if the very dust
was making sounds in its drifting,

as if the wind, barely perceptible,
whispered her secrets
through the cypress,
as if some star

in the far corner
of the window
suggested her color,
her unadvertised beauty.

Perhaps it's the quality
of the silence, the patience
of the listener that attracts her.
The promise that there are no nets.

A Perfect Day, Given The Sea

A perfect day, given the sea
not far from this window.
Today I accomplished very little
except for a bus ride for a date with an orange,
and a ten mile walk
up the hill to my house
and some pages from *The Fountain of Age*
while sipping some orange juice.
Watched a tennis star through a match
napped some, a low key perfect day
with the sea not far from this window.

Spring

Cottages,
tall weeds
hanging over windows,
old deteriorated barns
just passed the willows,

spring blossoms going wild
as if they all agreed
on time, color, the arch of their petals.
Already they are falling
as if the wind knew, the sky.

There is an art
to red winged blackbirds
flying over fields,
metallic voices
startling the afternoon

as if they too
knew
the blossoms,
places only a few
would have dared.

She Leaned Over

At some point
(I think 33,000 feet),
she leaned over and whispered
"Women are the superior race
don't you think"?
You agreed
wondering if the stewardess
wasn't a bit of an arch angel
as she poured more coffee
seeming to bless us.

She'd been seeing a man
named Wess for over a year
and Clay who flew her west
for the weekend who inherited
his fathers lumber business
who was much too serious.
A character fresh out of the pages
of F. Scott Fitzgerald's "Bernice Bobs Her Hair,"
or "The Offshore Pirate,"
who burst out laughing in regular intervals,

who said laughter was the only healer,
who wasn't planning on finding
anyone to blame as she started out
on her great journey,
who left me thinking life was much simpler,
much more interesting than most make it out to be.
Green eyes, faded black shirt,
a representative, an ambassador,
as if this were our own plane

and we had changed
the direction of the flight three or four times.
As if Clay and Wess and countless others
had forgotten how to sit and laugh,
stare in her eyes knowing
there wasn't anything they wanted, nothing
that couldn't be settled later
how in the face of death
(her green eyes, that mouth),
we're all strangers
seated on the same plane.

Jean

Out of the shower
just long enough to give coffee
making directions and you managed to find two cups
and most of what was needed.

You sat at her kitchen table
divided by a box of shredded wheat.
You told her she looked beautiful
(her long hair still wet from the shower)
and she said "What"?
And you didn't say anything
and she said "Thank you."

As you talked some rare January sunlight
played on the wood table
and a red and yellow turtleneck
hung over the back door.
She looked taller than she usually looks
sitting there.
She asked how the coffee was.
You said it was all right,
it had a kind of a bite to it
and she said coffee wasn't supposed
to have a bite to it
and you were silent for awhile.

She looks like the girl
who sat in front of you
in beginning Algebra
but there are countless settings
You could imagine her in.

You would like to say she had gray eyes
like the gray-eyed Athena
but there were actually various shades of green
depending on the light
and you could tell
what kind of mood she was in
just by looking over at them.
She had straight brown hair

she wore up occasionally
and an inclination towards satire.
A good consistent Leo,
almost the Leo they describe in astrology books:
generous, outward, in command, easily hurt.
You sat there remembering
how much she loved Johnny Mathis's
"Chances Are," slow dancing across carpets,
after the basketball game
in the basement in the corner
holding the one you hoped you would be holding.

High school
about the time Bob Dylan
was singing: "Tell yr ma, tell yr pa,
our loves gonna grow ow wa ow wa… "
And every once in a while
she'd see someone with hair
down to his shoulders
and wonder what that was all about.
No more complicated
than a few kisses,
how warm she could be…
the simplest of things.

THERE'S NO THERE THERE.
— Gertrude Stein

Your ghost at the counter writing a poem.
Next to you, realizing on a paper napkin
I'd forgotten to register for fall
laughing, delighted- that again,
I'd taken absolutely no
responsibility for myself.
A box of Shermans on the counter.

Cafe life.
I'd found paradise.
Escaped the nine to five,
trying to get ahead, tote that barge…
I'd somehow realized
there wasn't anything
worth the price.

Majoring in English literature
at a nearby field.
Discussing whether John Dunn, or the New Critics
or *Moll Flanders*
could equal the money
they were paying you
to return
in your late thirties.

Go back and sit in classrooms
just as spring was breaking,
look out windows — nothing but fields for miles.
Deep in the recesses of the cafeteria,
long conversations,

dark haired actresses who understood,
who had spent years studying
hoping to get the part.

John Dunn's "To a Coy Mistress."
The island.
Not that the form matters but the fire.
When you knew she knew.
The way she was sitting,
her laughter
Perhaps, she didn't know
and that was the real difficulty,

like you'd been speaking
Greek or Russian
she nodding, smiling…
Maybe you would take her
back with you to Greece.
Perpetually smoking,
drinking coffee, skipping class
like this was original, only once.

Lizard

It was the wind
and yes,
the highlight
of the day:
one there
in the pathway
in direct sunlight
watching me
watch him.

What does he see?
Another taller lizard
sunning himself
almost noon
searching for insects?
Perfectly still
(As if this was a law),
tilting his tiny head
upwards
to get
a better view,
to take all of me in.

NOVEL

Chapter One

That without releasing the fruits of one season, they cannot
    blossom into the next.
Sitting at a table approaching seven o'clock in the evening.
    Sitting at a table
repeating the word "yes" again and again. Yes to the night,
    being alive, yes to being
Married. Yes to sitting at a table approaching seven o'clock.

Chapter Two

The light on various faces, on a terrace in a cafe. All history
    is here now
the poem reads. A white BMW drives by — the poems are
    mainly recognitions
of death. Poetry's great subject: that we all die.

Chapter Three

"I wish, I wish, I wish in vein
that we would live happily in that room again
$10,000 at the drop of a hat
If our lives could be like that …
Laughin' and a Joken' till the early hours of the morn."*
                       — Bob Dylan

Chapter IV

Remember when it was only poetry. London, San Tropez,
    seeing the same moon Ezra
Pound saw over London, the royal ballet.

Chapter V

Rushing to the other side of town to her room. Her breasts,
    her smile.

Chapter VI

Mysticism: discovering the personal divine.
In search of the miraculous, figuring out the mystery.
Living the mystery. Life is not logic. Entering the unknown.
In silence there is a sacredness, a way of living differently.

February

Four birds flew by.
No telling where they are now.

The sea and the forest, clouds,
forgotten things,
Gods left alone.
Forests, parts of the sea.
Alone with these trophies.

The 7th Muse

In the shower
in the middle of the night.

The next morning
all the way to the village
and in the afternoon
in that room
while you moved
through unspeakable regions,
she told you with her eyes
it was perfectly ok
to be her lover.

This morning
in an apron years later
working the lunch shift
you nm into her.
Her long hair, green eyes,
her hands — nothing had changed
though a broken look on her face,
the way she talks.
How this obligation
must be met
and this.

Can almost see the tears
as she talks"Why am I working
in a kitchen"?
She seems to be saying
and you want to say "What's
wrong with working in a kitchen"?

you are still beautiful,
the sun is outside,
the earth is turning
not is one direction but two,
millions have lived out sagas,
loved and died on it.
Still a miracle
any of us can walk,
stand like characters
in some prize winning play.
Who convinced her
she was acting in the wrong play?
Some Madison Avenue copy writer
who continues to help
perpetuate this myth
that as long as you have money
(Ah…if only).
No matter that they die
in Beverly Hills daily
in the back of expensive homes
from drug overdoses
No matter that they jump off
balconies, expensive perfect balconies
connected to perfect homes,
unbeatable images.

No matter that the faces
of most of the successful
become their own traitors
to themselves
and nothing has mattered since.

He wanted her to know
there was a magic

behind the counter,
a dance in her green eyes
first cousin
to the little girl in her,
first cousin to the moon,
to the real despair
that has no trouble
playing anywhere.

THE DAY

Filled with movement
from bus to bus, cafe to cafe
lost in the blossoms along the roadside,
spring two days away.
Sitting in the back room now
with a view of the bay, trees
so still yet alive.
Wondering if the dead
have a way of contacting us:
the invisible.

Blue Corduroys

Inside the car, top on,
fresh french bread, cheese
black coffee in a paper cup,
a warm afternoon near the only cafe
I know she frequents in the afternoons.

Thinking about her long black hair,
her smell when I snuggled against her.
Her knees,
I kept telling myself
and how hard she was

and how she didn't care
and who walks by
in a white blouse and dark sunglasses
deliberately looking the other way,
the entire weight of the world

resting on her fragile shoulders,
blue corduroys.
She probably does remember
the only afternoon
we kissed.

Not one kiss but a dozen,
perhaps two dozen
the way memory selects certain sensations
you recall again and again…

Kneeling holding my face
in her hands,

lipstick smeared, afternoon sunlight,
half on the floor
all four of our legs
wrapped around each other
tangled up in black. hair,
as she walks past me now, slowly
(why look back, I think, why indeed).

The Moon

I wonder if the moon in Argentina
is any different than the moon in southern Sprain
or from my house
enclosed on two sides by apple trees.
Is it any different in the morning sky
(Which is when its at its most subtle),
paler than the faint blue morning
and only seen by luck.
I am convinced it is the same moon.

"We have shared out like thieves
the amazing treasure of nights and days."
— Borges

What is this? That they are hiddden…
Treasures more subtle than the moon
and so obvious they are out of reach,
hillsides, profiles of a face, words spoken
in a cafe, in months, years woven together
that would be impossible to define,
that could be measured in sunsets,
in the expression of a half dozen faces,
something like that moon in the late morning
that does not ask to be seen,
that is as pale as a lifetime.

VIII

A Foggy Day

A foggy day in January
Driving through the streets
She and I, an old Al Green song playing
Wondering if it could be this beautiful
The cold air, the heater,
"I should be with you till I die iiiiiiii …"

Rossell

I can see you with your blonde brown
hair curled to your neck.
In your new boots
and your new black wool coat
having a cafe lati
smiling, thinking about the gigantic grant
you'd just been awarded…
Which proves your beyond a journeyman
level grant writer at the very least.
Not to admit your cuteness
and its ranking in the county.

Love

First she takes off her glasses,
then her shoes.
She is so beautiful when she
climbs into bed.
Five feet eight and a half.
Brown hair.
What is there to say
except she's so desirable,
an Aquarius, her moon unknown.

Dancing

A full 24 piece orchestra all the old ballads.
A few new ones, it didn't matter: it was just
to hold her near, smell her light perfume
was all I wanted.
The next two or three days were like that
and then the magic set in
an unspoken love began creating itself
almost without our knowing it.

Brown green eyes, in a models frame,
she dazzles the imagination. Five eight,
She doesn't know how beautiful she is.
But who can blame her, most of us don't know.

Confession

Yes, it's Saturday, overcast
and I'm going to confess something:
all I've ever wanted
was the incredible…

It Wasn't So Much Dancing For Hours

It wasn't so much dancing for hours
that first night though holding someone
as attractive as she was … kissing her.
It's just that after thirty years
you can still remember her look
and why you fell in love.

With Or Without

He plods along
wondering how absolutely beautiful
everything is.
How perfect to be alive
to love and care.

The Sea

I've always loved the sea
its subtlety, it's mystery,
its color: the Italian, the Spanish,
the French sea-all delightful
romantic, wondrous backdrop
(the smell of it.)

July

I love summer
the warmth of it
the light and to be near you in summer
is almost more than I can bear.
To love in summer
is the best.
Like the ripe watermelon, cantaloupe
dripping down my cheeks…
Like the sun on the blue water, dazzling
like your arms tangled around me
To love in summer.
is the best.

www.ingramcontent.com/pod-product-compliance
Lightning Source LLC
Chambersburg PA
CBHW052101070526
44584CB00017B/2276